To- E ___ 's
from-
Aunt Margaret and Uncle Dick

P9-CSU-286

MY Frances Hook JESUS BOOK

© MCMLXII, The Standard Publishing Company

Stories by Wanda Hayes

ISBN 0-87239-239-2

Twenty-ninth Printing, 1990

©1963, The STANDARD PUBLISHING Company, Cincinnati, Ohio • Printed in U.S.A.

The Mother of Jesus

Long ago there was a young woman named Mary. She was a very good woman.

One day God sent an angel to Mary. She must have been surprised to have an angel visit her, for the angel said to her, "Do not be afraid, Mary."

Then the angel told Mary, "God is very pleased with you. He has chosen you to be the mother of a very special baby boy. His name will be Jesus. He will be God's own Son."

After the angel spoke, Mary was so happy that she wanted to sing. "I will be very glad to be the mother of Jesus," she said.

Mary knew God would help her to be a good mother. She may have prayed, "Thank you, God," for this good news.

Story from Luke 1:26-38

© MCMLXII, The Standard Publishing Company

Baby Jesus

Mary and her husband, Joseph, came to the city of Bethlehem. There were so many people in Bethlehem that Mary and Joseph had to sleep in a stable. Cows and sheep lived in the stable. But there was room for Mary and Joseph. And there was soft, warm hay to lie down on.

"Ummm, the hay smells sweet," said Mary.

"I am glad to have a nice place to rest," said Joseph.

That night in the warm stable in Bethlehem, a baby boy was born to Mary. He was the special baby boy God had promised. Mary wrapped Him in soft cloth and laid Him in a manger filled with soft, warm hay.

"Hello, baby Jesus," said Mary and Joseph.

"Baa, baa," said the sheep softly.

Baby Jesus was asleep.

Story from Luke 2:1-7

MCMLXII, The Standard Publishing Company

Happy Shepherds

On a grassy hillside some shepherds were taking care of sheep. They did not want the sheep to get lost. They did not want a wolf to hurt the sheep.

Suddenly there was a shining angel standing by the shepherds. They were afraid.

"Don't be afraid," said the angel. "I have good news to make everybody in the world happy. Tonight in Bethlehem Jesus has been born. You will find Him wrapped in soft clothes and lying in a manger."

And suddenly there were many, many angels. They said a special thank you to God because Jesus was born.

When the angels were gone, the men who took care of the sheep weren't afraid any more. "Let's go see the baby the angel told us about." And they hurried as fast as they could.

After the shepherds saw the baby Jesus sleeping in the manger, they said special thank-yous to God. They were very happy.

Story from Luke 2:8-20

© MCMLXII, The Standard Publishing Company

A Visit to the Temple

Mary picked up Jesus from the bed where He had been sleeping. She wrapped Him in new, clean clothes. Today was a special day for the baby Jesus. Today Joseph and Mary would take Him for a visit. They would take Him to the temple.

The temple was shiny and clean. It was almost like a church building. In one part some people were praying. In another part some people were singing to God.

Mary and Joseph made a promise at the temple. They said, "We will take good care of Jesus. We will teach Him to love and obey God."

God heard Mary and Joseph's promise. God knew Mary and Joseph would take good care of His Son, Jesus.

Story from Luke 2:22

© MCMLXII, The Standard Publishing Company

A Happy Mother

Mary held little baby Jesus in her arms. She thanked God many times for choosing her to be Jesus' mother.

Mary felt very happy to be the mother of God's own Son. She took very good care of baby Jesus. She fed Him. She rocked Him in her arms so He could go to sleep. She may have sung songs to Him to make Him happy.

Mary watched everything that Jesus did. Jesus grew just as you did when you were a baby. Sometimes He laughed, and sometimes He cried. Sometimes He kicked His feet.

Mary may have held Jesus close to her every day and said, "I love you, baby Jesus."

Baby Jesus felt very happy in His mother's arms.

Story from Luke 2:40

© MCMLXII, The Standard Publishing Company

A Good Son

The first time Jesus went to the temple, He was a little baby. After that visit, Jesus and Mary and Joseph lived in Nazareth. And God blessed Jesus. He grew and became strong. And He was very wise.

At last Jesus was twelve years old. "Today is the day, Jesus," said His mother. "Today you may go with Joseph and me to worship in the temple."

Jesus was glad that He could go to the temple and pray to God just as Mary and Joseph had done when He was a little baby.

It took many days to go to Jerusalem. Jesus was very glad to be there. Most of all He was glad to be in the temple worshiping God. Jesus prayed to God for He liked to talk to His Father in heaven.

Jesus obeyed God. He obeyed Mary and Joseph. Jesus was a good son. Mary and Joseph were pleased with Him. And God was pleased with His Son.

Story from Luke 2:41-52

© MCMLXII, The Standard Publishing Company

The Woman by a Well

After Jesus grew to be a man, He traveled all around the country teaching the people about His Father, God. Jesus' friends went with Him. They walked along the hot, dusty roads.

One day when Jesus and His friends had walked for a long time, they stopped at a well to rest.

A Samaritan woman came to fill her pitcher. Jesus was thirsty. He said to the woman, "Give me a drink."

The woman was surprised. "Why do you speak to me—someone you don't even know?" she asked.

"If you knew who I am, you would have asked me for something," Jesus said, "something much better than a drink of water."

Jesus and the woman talked for a long time. And Jesus told the woman many things about herself. All the time Jesus was talking, the woman may have been thinking, "I know He is someone great." Then the woman said to Jesus, "I know that God promised to send Jesus, who will tell us everything."

Jesus must have looked at the woman very kindly as He said, "I am Jesus."

The woman had found something much better than water. She found Jesus, God's own Son.

Story from John 4:5-26

© MCMLXII, The Standard Publishing Company

"Thank You"

Wherever Jesus went people said, "Please make me well." And Jesus did. He made blind people see. He made lame people walk. He made dead people alive. The people knew God's Son could do these things.

One day as Jesus and His friends started to go into a city, they heard some men call, "Jesus, teacher, help us." Jesus saw ten men who were very sick. They had bad sores on their bodies.

Jesus told them, "Go, show yourselves to the priests." The men did what Jesus said, and as they started to walk away they looked at their bodies. The sores were all gone. Jesus made all ten men well. How happy they were!

Nine of the men hurried on into the city to show their friends they were well. But one man came running back to Jesus. He lay down on the ground at Jesus' feet and said, "Thank you, Jesus. Thank you for making me well."

Jesus was sorry that nine of the men didn't say "thank you." But He was very glad that one man did. Jesus knew this man really loved Him.

Story from Luke 17:11-19

© MCMLXII, The Standard Publishing Company

A Kind Shepherd

One time Jesus told this story: "There was a shepherd who took care of one hundred sheep. Early in the morning he led them out of their fold into the fields.

"The shepherd loved to walk with his sheep through the fields where they could eat soft, green grass. He loved to sit by a cool stream of water where the sheep could get a drink. 'Baa, baa,' said the daddy and mama sheep. 'Maa, maa,' said the baby lambs.

"When the day was almost over, the shepherd took his sheep back to the fold. As they went in the gate, he counted them, 'One, two, three, . . .' all the way up to ninety-nine. That's all there were. One sheep was gone.

"The kind shepherd closed the gate and went to find his lost sheep. He looked in the big grassy field. He looked by the stream. He climbed up the rocky hillside. 'I'm coming,' he called.

"Soon the shepherd found the poor, scared sheep. He lifted him very carefully to his shoulder. 'I will take you back home now.'

" 'Baa, baa,' said the sheep. 'Thank you.'

"The sheep was very happy, but the shepherd was happiest of all."

Story from Luke 15:3-6

© MCMLXII, The Standard Publishing Company

A Man in a Tree

"Jesus is coming."

"The Master is coming," all the people were saying. They were excited. Soon everybody knew that Jesus was in their city. Men and women, boys and girls crowded along the street to see Jesus.

"I want to see Jesus, too," thought Zacchaeus. "But all of these tall people are in front of me, and I am too short to see over their heads." Zacchaeus was a very short man. "I have heard so many wonderful things about Jesus," said Zacchaeus. "I must see Him."

Zacchaeus looked around. "I know how I can see Jesus." And he climbed a tall tree by the street.

Zacchaeus looked far down the street. Several men were coming. One of them was Jesus. Soon He would walk right under the tree where Zacchaeus was. But Jesus didn't walk by the tree. Instead He stopped underneath it, and He looked up at Zacchaeus. Jesus looked up at him and said, "Zacchaeus, hurry and come down for I'm going to stay at your house today."

Zacchaeus did hurry down from the tree, and Jesus and His friends did stay at Zacchaeus' house that day. Zacchaeus was very glad he climbed the tree to see Jesus.

Story from Luke 19:1-10

© MCMLXII, The Standard Publishing Company

Jesus and the Children

"Go to Jesus," said the mothers. "Go with the other children."

Jesus was sitting on a large stone. He saw the mothers bringing their little babies to Him. He saw other boys and girls coming to Him. Jesus loved them.

But Jesus' helpers stood in front of Him and said, "Don't bring the children to Jesus today. He is tired. Let Him rest. Go back to your mothers, children. Go on now. Leave Jesus alone."

Jesus did not like what His helpers said. He said to them, "Let the children come to me. Don't stop them."

And the children ran to Jesus. He asked God to bless each one of them. Then Jesus put His hand on each little boy and each little girl. He put His arms around them. Jesus smiled at one little girl as He held her face with His hands. "I love you, Jesus," she said.

Story from Matthew 19:13-15
and Mark 10:13-16

© MCMLXII, The Standard Publishing Company

A Song for Jesus

It was a special day in Jerusalem. Jesus was coming to worship in the temple. When the people heard Jesus was coming, they went out to meet Him. They spread their coats down on the road. These made a special carpet for Him to ride on—just like a king. Some of the people cut branches from trees and laid them in the road for Jesus.

Then Jesus came riding on a donkey. There were many, many people. They were so glad that they shouted, "Hosanna to the son of David. Hosanna in the highest." This was how they showed Jesus they loved Him. This was how they said, "We know you are very great."

Jesus got off His donkey and walked into the temple. Many sick people came to Him, and He made them well. And all the time He was in the temple, Jesus heard the children singing to Him, "Hosanna to the son of David. Hosanna!" The children knew Jesus was their friend. He liked their song.

Story from Matthew 21:6-11, 14-16

© MCMLXII, The Standard Publishing Company

A Lesson Jesus Taught

Jesus and Peter and John and Jesus' other friends were eating together. After supper Jesus did something His friends had never seen Him do. He took a towel. He took a pitcher and poured clean water into a bowl. Jesus' friends watched everything that He did.

"What is He going to do?" they may have said to each other. Soon they knew.

Jesus began to wash His helpers' feet with the water and dry them with the towel. That was a good thing for Him to do because their feet got dirty walking along the dusty roads. The cool water felt very good.

When Jesus washed Peter's feet, Peter said, "Why are you washing my feet?" Peter didn't think Jesus should do a job like that because He was God's own Son.

After Jesus washed the feet of all His friends there, He sat down again and answered Peter's question. "I have washed your feet to teach you to do kind things for each other and for other people."

Jesus' friends did obey Him. They were kind to each other. They were kind to other people, too. And they always remembered the time Jesus washed their feet.

Story from John 13:3-17

© MCMLXII, The Standard Publishing Company

The Good News

Jesus' friends were very sad. They thought they would never see Jesus again. They thought they would never be happy again.

One morning Mary and some other friends of Jesus heard the good news. The women heard that they would see Jesus again. They ran to tell the good news to other friends of Jesus.

Suddenly the women stopped because someone was standing in front of them. It was Jesus! The women could hardly believe that Jesus was really there. But He talked to them. He said, "Tell my friends that I will meet them soon."

The women worshiped Jesus. They were happy that Jesus had come back to see them.

Story from Matthew 28:1-10

© MCMLXII, The Standard Publishing Company

A Prayer by Jesus

Jesus was God's own Son, and He talked to God the way we do. He prayed to Him. Jesus prayed to His Father every day.

One day Jesus walked along a road with two of His friends. He talked with them about the Old Testament. The men loved to hear Jesus teach. They listened to everything He said.

When Jesus and the two men came to the city, one of the men said, "Come and eat supper with us."

Jesus probably said, "Thank you," because they invited Him to stay with them.

Before the men ate, Jesus bowed His head and thanked God for the food as He always did. Perhaps He said, "Thank you for this bread, my Father. Thank you for my kind friends."

And Jesus' friends may have said, "Thank you, heavenly Father, for Jesus."

Story from Luke 24:13-15, 28-30

MCMLXII, The Standard Publishing Company

Our Best Friend Is Jesus

© MCMLXII, The Standard Publishing Company

1. My best friend is Je - sus, Love Him, love Him,
2. My best friend is Je - sus, Thank Him, thank Him,

My best friend is Je - sus, I love Him.
My best friend is Je - sus, I thank Him.

Words and music by Mildred A. Stagg.
From *Songs We Sing.* Copyright, 1939, Broadman Press.